I0581129

WHEN SHE BECAME YOU / SONGS TO SUZANNE

WHEN SHE BECAME YOU / SONGS TO SUZANNE

Michael Jennings

Copyright © 2022 by Michael Jennings. All Rights Reserved.

ISBN 978-1-7338882-9-5

Acknowledgement: Special thanks to Darryl Hughto for permission to use his painting "La Casa" on the cover. His images also inspired several of the poems in the opening section "Where She Dances."
—MJ

Manufactured in the United States of America

Black Spruce Press
blacksprucepress.org
blacksprucepress@gmail.com
Design by forgetgutenberg.com

The past was terrible. I sat beside myself
near the river of bones. The low hanging
leaves called to me, threatening my waters.
I pretended not to be listening. I killed
the river's fish, picked tree bark. I said
to myself, this is my hand, this is my eye,
and this the world I bring to my mouth.
But who is that tree moving like water,
who is that dark and smooth shining water
growing into your eyes, becoming the smell
of moss in the palms of your hands. And why
does it mirror my hand, my mouth, my eye?
>*So all day now, I paint you, sing you, see you.*
>*I give you a home in the bones of the mountain.*

WHERE SHE DANCES

Where She Dances

Purple jaguar midnight
of lost imaginings—ebony, jet,
obsidian lakes of fire—
hers are the drumbeat spanking of bare
hard feet, far off wafting of laughter.

Come dance with the daughter
of rag-tag summer. See the turn
of her fiery wrist. Moon
paints her shadow. Sun
cannot find her. The fierce stars

bring her to bliss.
Once she was tree trembling in moonlight.
Once she was river
tied down by her hair.
Once she was wind, once she was breath—

now only flame
in the flare
of a pupil,
a delicate rustle's
velvety purr.

When the River Flutters

her wings, she is no longer the Amazon
floating the crescent moon as her navel,

she is your shadow rising to meet you.
The nightsilk mountains bend close.

Something in the lisping silence grieves,
exalts, dies its thousand deaths.

Your body is also a river with wings,
with talons, a place of betrayals

where shadowy gods, horned
or with twisting serpents for hair

are drowned, torn to shreds,
then rise again into stars.

Tomorrow, at dawn,
something shaggy will come down,

peering out from the night-drugged leaves,
dazzled by the spokes of new sun.

Her Dalliance

Between her fingers
the plucked stalk of your brainstem
blossoms

petal by petal in the empty air.
Between her toes
Tigris and Euphrates divide

and multiply. She loves you.
She loves you not.
Perhaps you are the pinprick rain

on the sheer face of an autumn lake.
Perhaps you are snow.
She is dreaming of crossroads

and you are the emptiness.
She is playing with dolls
and you are the mad muttering.

She is gossiping by the well
and you are the strewn fieldstones,
lidless eyes of the desert

waiting for rain. Her indecision
is delicious with cunning.
The mountains heave. Your leaves shiver.

When She Makes Mountains

she paints them shadow-dancing,
        rivers their flexions,
weaves the drapery wind. Dozes.

        Crosses into dream-space
with long-thighed stepping, her sleep-heat
 burnishing the low hills.

Out of them come women for water,
        bright as flowers, a dozen Salomes
with braceleted ankles and hard brutal feet

        who crouch on their haunches
under the thick scent of limes, their mud village
        creviced above them,

its brown face among the cliffs
        immobile as a blind man's.
She breathes them her gossip,

        whiskers their thighs,
puts the wheels of their hips
        in slow motion. Jars

grow from their heads, jars
        in the shape of women
heedless in May, the time of new grasses.

Sometime Before Words Perhaps

your arm moved—
a glitter of small hinges.
Or was it your leg,
its calculated unwinding?

I was asleep, say,
or lost in thought.
I heard your blood
though, how it sang,

and I felt your cloud-shadow
coming, crossing my face.
I looked—
you were full of yourself

dancing. I looked—
you were the waterfall of yourself
dancing. I looked—
your breath drank my eyes.

I listened—your feet drummed
shut my ears. I groped
but your skin turned fingers
to spider webs.
              Sometime,
out of the dark of my body
I spoke.

Today Perhaps the Lizard

who lies down in his own shadow,
inventing the sun through half-closed eyes,
feels his skin, thickening with years,
grow nervous as water.
Perhaps he just feels lucky.

You keep coming back like a dream.
Your hips make light shiver,
make me peer up silly-sideways
like an old dog
to watch the bonfire of your bones.

Night's coming, though.
The sky-blue water
of your eyes will turn dark
then. Stars will come out.

Tomorrow
you will come and go again
like a river—
your bright bones
                stealing my shadow.

At Twilight

Fatherless among the animals I wake in the half-light,
sinless as a June bug, pure as Narcissus.
I am what I look at.
The leaves see me and know my smell.
What I touch touches me back.

I cannot know whether I am the flower
or the flower of the flower
or just smooth water
reflecting tree more ravishing than tree,
flower more wayward than flower,

when your witch-light comes like gossamer
brushing my cheek.

FOR YOU I INVENT THE SUN

For You I Invent the Sun

1.

This, of course, is what money won't buy, this
hip-to-hip, two-centered circle, drift
and drift—you in front, provocative
as a pomegranate, me in front, hearing
echoes—your footsteps filling mine
the way perhaps snow fills the tracks
of caribou, keeping the wolves off. We're
birds of a feather. Our minds veer
and arc on the same air. It's open season here
on sun and wind, and I'm wearing my license
conspicuous and on my sleeve.

2.

We scuff and boot the leaves like six-year-olds,
grin like raccoons. *These are years,* we say,
*shed like snake skins—doomed, irrelevant,
beautiful.* Miles or years, we've walked
forever here, you and I, putting on
or shedding each other like light or leaves,
the traffic hushed and distant. We feel exotic
as the names of these lakeshore towns we walk in,
the water quiet, leaves falling, the light quixotic.
It's all new. You're new—taut and muscular
as a spring colt claiming his first field.
I'm new—grinning ear to ear, hearing windmills.
Death is new here, too, and moves like water underfoot.

3.

We drift in October light through the rose garden,
all the roses gone. Clothed in purple and black,
you're naked. Naked, raspberries and cream,

you're clothed. It's magic. For you I invent the sun,
feel tragic, drive it to your doorstep
in a long yellow cab, stand there, hat in hand,
like some foolish figure in a thirties' flick—

your hair darker than any back-row seat.

4.

You talk, stoop, pick weeds, say *the sky
has breadth.* I say *birds have scissored
it to death,* but I'm dazzled anyway.
It's late fall. The birds look hungrier.
You say you're leaving your husband anyhow—
for all his good, for all my bad.
Standing against a tree, your hood up,
your half-moon smile floating somewhere
below the hairline, I imagine you grew there
whole, yesterday perhaps, dew-like, and I
kiss you, feel shy, boyish—hungry
the way the old birds must
who know they won't get south.

5.

It's mid-winter and the crunching underfoot
sounds rare, precious. You're
purple and yellow. I'm fatigue L.L. Bean
gray green. The six years between us though
is hardly May and January,
and I'm dazzled by purple and yellow
and can outrun you anyway.
You admit now, though, cold hurts,
for all your tough talk. I should admit
what...for all my tough talk?—that my wife
writes, calls, cries, argues, accuses? Indeed
this crunching underfoot *is* precious—glass

or ice. It's January. It will soon
be May. Our rooms are white and beautiful
and bloom with plants.

6.

Your mother calls, sends chocolates, prays—
makes me feel like the anti-Christ. And
it's true enough I come from a land
of sand and stone, and never put much trust
in trees or green. (In my mind's eye
I always return
to the same rock ridge, almost abstract now
in the blind revision of its lie—
a dark sawblade raised against blue sky.)
But here, your walk is so much like the sun
or prayer, I must stoop
and touch the place you've stepped, knowing
come spring, something will grow there.

7.

Today bright sun makes blue sky and white birds
pure blue, pure white, barely visible
as we squint and almost stumble
in the pure light.
                    Yet we feel entitled here
as tourists, say, who've paid their fare,
though never dreaming it would look like this.
Beguiled by the low cant of foreign tongues,
we're half afraid some blunt truth in our own talk
will startle us back to earth, bring the dream
crashing like glass about our ears.
                                But this
is mid-March,
                when the wind blows and the domed sky
holds,

when small nests of clustered stones
nosing into wind on the iced canal
rise and become birds.
                            This is the season
of the long white distance,
                                    when seeing
is much like blindness, blindness like pure sight.

8.

You say, *You are the magician, I but the source.*
Who could top that? Who, mid-stride,
could help but feel the joy
of fear stutter his heart
like cloud-shadow. We have walked
a long time. It is growing dark. I wish
to take you in my arms. I wish to say
to the child we will one day make,
You grew here, among sun and wind
in the gathering dark. I wish to say,
Your mother was taken
for goddess
among stones, among these circling
and calling birds,
                        and they were not far wrong.

9.

We have, I think, no word for this thin-aired
quiet full of light, through which we drift
like new ghosts
risen to Elysian Fields—the still, green lakes
somnolent as deep thought. It's the day
before Easter. The fishermen
standing on the firm bank
wave their fly-rods like bright wands
toward dark depths

where once new life must have climbed, sloth-like
into a dream of sunlight,
and where now loud children and willing dogs
are all smiles, wagging tongues,
sinew and muscle.
Today we talk less, think more.
Today we smile at all that is sensuous
and literal.

I See You Bend Down

in the garden of pain, the garden of spring,
your after-frost loam-blackened fingers
rooted in roots, dreaming the furred shoots
and delicate unfoldings
of dewy lipped angels attuned to the stars,

and some jungle in me starts growing,
some man of leaves gone slitty-eyed
with cunning, who scans the sky
for a new pale moon

to catch tonight
in the arms of the hairy
old forest—
          dark mangrove, tall cypress.

Always

under the leaves there was death waiting,
despite your tuned, high-voltage body.

Tigers and rivers glide in us nameless
though the day fades and it is never enough.

The poem deconstructing was an old saw
but we made honey in its warm caldron

and I said love with the white mouth
of the moonflower, with iridescent suns

of coneflowers flaunting whispery black eyes.
It was summer in the garden where you moved

without burden of self like a cloud, paused,
looked, shifting your glorious haunches

like any happy horse claiming its field—
all heat and hunger and applause.

River Time

The hills are green with summer,
the lakes cobalt blue and glittering.
Whatever we longed for in March
is here already or forgotten.
Your hair gleaming obsidian
as always, despite a few white renegades,
your body stretches out like a great cat's
or a landscape I never tire of crossing.
When I kiss the small of your back,
I hear the whisper of desert sands,
the rush of young rivers. No one comes back.
No one steps twice in the same body.
Spring was sun on the daffodils
and the time of the new wide sky,
the heart-breaking golds
of the giant willows.
Marry me, marry me
shouted the cardinal in his tall tree
while the goldfinch giggled
I am nothing but light.

INVOCATIONS

Invocations

My steps slower than I would have imagined
even in summer

who once could not help but run
Crimes I've done myself I would not undo

Cicadas in a tree singing
the dappled 'out there'

the shrill of birdsong

*   *   *   *

Sands of the desert and sun warm me
and I forgive my pederast father
and remember his shy laugh

Spawn of East Texas swamps snakes on the train
Stink of rot and piney woods loneliness
Bible-belt mom dowsed in lavender

I had an engineer's hat like my grandfather's
high in the sun-flared locomotive squinting into the light

the two of us until the whistle blew
and he was a crouched old man on a hospital inner tube

My father's bones shattered like glass and he died
worse than a dog so I forgave him

remembering his shy laugh glints of gold
in his long old teeth
Two funny stories maybe three and no one knew him
His skull in death an old Ojibwa's

*   *   *   *

At night the familiar hocus pocus of moon and mind
You soft in shadow that other
I know myself by

Come Light warm me
Sit on my grandmother's shoulder
who reads me through measles and chickenpox
bringing the world and New Orleans
in two blue suitcases

Light on the banana tree tallest of grasses
Light in her hazel eyes

*   *   *   *

Salt sand of the desert the long unfolding white of it
Out there I stole my bride from the land of the untouch-
ables
Spirit me away dawn of the cockcrow
Light of my wavering window

*   *   *   *

My one great photograph you naked on a chaise lounge
eight months pregnant sleeping in the sun
light circling your circles
and one long draped arm

Light of the moment and always

*   *   *   *

Our son came out a greased chicken when he was born
and shone in the light of all subsequent Christmases

He seemed too small to take home
I had to learn to hold his head up

26

Your breasts engorged made you the gaudy
fertility goddess carved on a wooden salad spoon
I remembered from childhood

I gave him his first bath
Danced him heart to heart
Happy on the high hill of our summer

*   *   *   *

And happily I am already dead in a book somewhere
but in the dark closed pages or the light of a window
I don't know

To think I was ever a blank page
a tabula rasa a salt flat
a star

Hold the light at the window I am coming
though my knees ache

*   *   *   *

I have always enjoyed near the Equator
how sun maps a face
though I live in the snow

I was young in the sun of tennis courts
Pure form and goat mind
fencing the air
before the flat-light green-haze of hospitals
moon men in surgeries
Mother a mirage in the midnight
arriving from Rome

Stars of Paris outside my window
The girl I held in the dark for 13 years
against my loneliness

swims in the sun of the Pacific now
or is dead

*   *   *   *

I made love on a red cliff over the Mediterranean
at midnight in the cove of Los Pinos
to a woman from another language
beautiful as a mermaid
and hairy as a 23-year-old
I was young dumb in a hurry
No star touched my soul

*   *   *   *

When I think of light I think of salt flats or snow
though its jewels in the leaves are delectable
and fire your black hair

All these summers I've watched you garden our gold hill
Your hillocks not bad Old Woman
raised like prayer
Names of flowers elude me unless I look them up
Is it the desert in me or a dark mind
that cannot name these belles of light

My first garden was elephant ears and banana trees
and blunt nosed tortoises I kissed on their blunt noses
mossy bricks of the patio
a slight breeze I still recall
on my heat-rashed two-year-old naked buttocks

At three and a ward of the Church
I wanted to bathe with the Deacon's
13-year-old daughter Mary Katherine
because I liked her pubic hair
how it swirled in the warm water

One or two baths and everyone thought better of it
From then on it was Morgan or Hank

And still my life seems strange
I think my lake the Danube sometimes
or remember the pale lime-thick turquoise of the
        Karoon River
an eel under my left foot
in a shock of wonder

Salt flats and snow and the gardens between

*   *   *   *

Wherever it was light wanted to go
I said Yo Dis here is America
Let's do-si-do
Dat old Walt Whitman he big he kind
but boring

Which tribe am I
The twang the drawl the Yankee clipper
Which thrum of weathers
Which codes and netherworlds
Which beestings on the tongue

Or is the eye my alibi
and crude syntax

*   *   *   *

The eye that travels
sees still waves from airplanes
thunderless beaches

In the border towns
of the dead and nearly dead
comes dawn's bleak windows

The casualties were
entirely justified
say the generals

And all that flat line clarity is light
But what of the gutturals of evening
the festooned flesh and ornamental slang
the topsy-turvy muscles of a million mutabilities
carnal carnivals and carnivores
boardwalk bazaar bodega
heartstrings of the tongue's thrumming
when light of the blood is a kind of light

*   *   *   *

I drummed through the booze jungles of Bangkok
at age 15 door to door whore to whore
till one just 17 took me home to meet the folks
and wash me in the kitchen sink
It was intimate chilling a grim mirror
and in the sickly light of the bare bulb
she was truly beautiful
How much of her may have wished to dance
on my grave I don't know

*   *   *   *

Angels and vaginas the angels are
vaginas says my sculptor friend in his studio
when I find his new seraphim
stock and static

Stepping back I see it
Yes
if thighs had wings surely we could fly

From a dark declivity a few curlings
broadening into fern fronds
and baroque arabesques
a vertical mouth for a trunk
and the tree of life is any man's wife

*   *   *   *

And then there were the horses of the sun
ablaze over the clattering rooftops of the world
or at least Khuzistan with its rock hills
and smugglers' trails
A heartbeat between the knees
A breathing like the very wind
Flying the flags of themselves in their girlish manes
the foolishness of all our fathers in their wild eyes

In a monoprint I bought from a friend
three horses graze in a pasture
that might be cloud
the passionless horses of dream or a far field
closer to me now than the horses of wind and fire
muscle and bone
though I miss their salt scent
the rivers of sweat mapping the veins of their necks

Or maybe my friend's print is a dream of horses
dreaming their pastures dreaming their clouds
dreaming the artist dreaming of horses
whose absence is light
around the dark remembered bodies

*   *   *   *

When my horse the fastest in all Khuzistan died
I was away at college and knew in an instant
my childhood had ended

I tried writing a poem
but couldn't get the Braille of his skin
under my fingers onto the page
He'd lent me the great thunder of his body
and I had lain on his flanks in his stall while he slept
We loved each other with humor like brothers
On the day of our triumph he had blown by
Star of Persia to win by 20 lengths
He nickered and snorted when he heard my footsteps
and when I did not come for months he died
His life blessed mine as only animals can bless
Sometimes our betrayals are mindless as wind
and a man moves emptier than the child that had been

*   *   *   *

Moon of my mind with your long black hair
Come nearer sit opposite
Let me paint you the girl in the rattan chair
one full breast exposed
one knee drawn up that hides the other
A portrait in shadow but the light of the room

Or now the wise handsome woman Penelope old
whom Odysseus fears taking his eyes off
in his fog of years
The firm cool cheek and coolish eyes
and fires that flicker at night
along her spine

Flesh is not sexy to an old man's eye
until defied by gravity the slightly
slipped buttocks that affirms some pride
the waist loosening its stays
that still has grace
the back that arches that's known some ache
Of course it helps he knew the girl

entwined back in that Ithacan Eden world
neither of them doin nothin
that wouldn't make her mama's hair curl

*   *   *   *

The song of the desert is the song of oases
the white sand and midnight blue
of Persian Miniatures
In college I took the Luscher Color Test
"not a party game" we played
as a party game

The colors you chose showed your balance of mind
the book said and I got four asterisks
which meant not even with psychological counseling
would my mind be right

I saw the cultural bias of course
bright yellow and cool green
being the colors of Switzerland on a nice day

I chose burnt orange and a warm brown
the colors "only refugees" had chosen
the colors of Iranian cliff towns

Third I chose a dark blue
which meant according to the book
I used sex to block my fears
of various underworlds and my sense of doom

O well
The pipes of Pan play
as the pipes of Pan do

And it was a midnight blue
the color of oases
the cry of loons

*   *   *   *

In a glaze of light
the desert men of the high plateau
have faces like worn shoes
Descendants of Alexander's men
their gazes impassive over wide valleys
their stories as cadenced
as Omar Khayyam

Goats jangling like temple bells
they take tea in a circle
talk with their hands
haggling the prices of horses

I know nothing of their wives
or daughters
shadowy sometimes giggly in the doorways

*   *   *   *

No massing of light on a sundown cliff face
was ever more magical than the changing light
in our son's face

The garden gnome crouching at your side
primed to know name and each thrilling step
of each new planting his voice
of query and awe a small
very silvery bell

His little collie Tommy carved trails
into our deep thickets and taught him the woods

quail raccoon an occasional fox
a big black stray he glowered down
like the wrath of God
He died on one of those trails on a sunny day
at just age 10 with a single yelp
Our son's wail like a knife in the heart
lasted forever

What could I teach him the world
is sometimes like a poem but mostly isn't
Distrust money men corporate slogans pompous diction

The larger he grew the smaller I seemed

Now he has sideburns like Jim Bowie
and slouches in the sun where he walks

We hope he'll learn to think

*   *   *   *

I wanted to write a poem
whose first line anticipated its last
a box of inevitability
an inevitable box

But life is not like that
Life is a Bob Dylan song
that might go anywhere
or become mumbly and indecipherable
Tramps train whistles a bad sky

We wait for the refrain
Buzzards are circling the bad sky
Tramps enter the train whistles
and then the far blue mountains

But we have faith
Beauty is also circling we think
We wait for the refrain

*   *   *   *

And there you are again in the garden
after long winter and long years
your sports car body our chiropractor
complains you treat like a truck
your mud wife duds a swatch of black earth
glazing your forehead
radiant
pensive
dreaming garden again out of the squalor
of sticks and mud the sprawled
scrawled skeletons
There's no light I'd rather enter
than this sun on our porch in late March
the bare trees on the far hills rusting with inner fires
the lake ice jagged and scarred
and about to vanish

And we could vanish too Love
become wolves on our ancient hill
our tails still plumed and playful
our eyes still fires

a little blood on the sumac leaves
their wands waving toward a new autumn

LAMENTATIONS

Lament 1

I sat on the edge of my bed and I wailed and I wept
and I wanted to be empty as wind
and avoid all this old man dying shit
all this piecemeal dissolution humiliation
I wanted to rise like the Phoenix like the sun
and be new in the morning like the sun
I wanted to be 56 forever everything still
almost possible you like a mirage
just ahead within reach a rainbow's
shimmering I wanted to walk in
content in my fate to be walking still walking
the ache in my knees both telling and reassuring
and you in the paper tiara from the party
Queen May aswirl in the ribbons of mock death
and resurrection and I knew making love
to you would make me whole through the universe
and everything else the denouement the terrible
     denouement
weeping and keening holding the rags the bitter rags
and then I was empty as wind and quiet

Lament 2

I went to the place of the poem but it was small
and dark and smelled like the ancient dens of foxes
Time kept coming back to scratch at the door
Old words littered the walls as if to keep the damp out
Someone had lit a fire but the ashes were cold
and the spiders were everywhere
And there was such sadness in the spaces between words
so much nothingness in the everything they said
Why fear the nothingness but we do
How fear the meaninglessness which we are
Here is my voice hang it on a tree
Here is my shoe which remembers me
And beautiful were your black diamonds
like the beauty of the sea at night
the points and spires and breezes of the night
where you passed and I followed and the words went out
and I vanished

Lament 3

I wanted to steal the last word from Death I suppose
and the silkiest of thefts are the poems of moonlight
poems of the sea and vast deserts their premonitions
And yet the Angel of Death is all kindness we're told
leading us out into moonlight through cracks in the
     clouds
had we known had we listened as the terrible talons
of pain and undoing let go
                              let us pray let us hope
the last ravening moments no end of consciousness
but a beginning
                  let us hope let us pray
though your buttocks domes against my limp gizmo
are all I need tonight to shore me home

Lament 4

How shall I say goodbye to myself poor
Charles Bon in his New Orleans and his emptiness
his decadence and charm and poisonous knowledge
who yet found you beyond all luckiness or fate
Goodbye to the heart hurt by its own betrayals
the mind full of inconsequence and error
a voice too full of itself
knickknacks and charms and the color blue
the silent cries of trees and the lake's sheen
and the numberless leaves haunting the numbered days
The man of the hour is the skeleton in the sombrero
who lies down in the curves of the voluptuous senorita
to a clatter of bedpans in the wings and the cackling of
        the damned
I sang you the songs of your fiery bones
and the soft opening flower of a dying kiss
Farewell to the grief of days and the holy smell of roses
your face knees voice like water
thighs like snow and eyes full of sky
Your laugh startled me so so so long ago
My will such as it is I give to clouds and to dreaming
my bones to the cathedrals of sand
to the pottery shards of lost places
my eyes to the vulture who resembles me
my wishes to wind and my loneliness
to thousand-year-old trees and the deserts of desire
I loved you in the simplest of ways my girl
and this is my poem which has no ending

Lament 5

I can imagine the loneliness of widows unraveling
unwelcoming days and old men in shut rooms
measuring their meds losing their minds dates names
If only vanishing were easy an old movie maybe
the corny deathbed speech the melodrama
each bedside mourner a cameo and case study
You see it in the eyes the soul speaking eye to eye
for the last time drinking the last horizon
And the faces strange and the rooms we wake in
with a start the floor moving and the windows dark
are no more ours than the clouds are or the voices of
    children
Is it the book misplaced that makes me weep
or tortured animals slaughtered children rape
by bayonet or any gone world's going
My grandmother kept a book 85 years pressing
a four-leaf clover given by a friend when they were five
Isn't that worth more than walking on the moon
but nothing stays still straight or in place
but the mute dignity of bones
bones without memory bones without song
So let us go under the hill and over the sky
and let us be bones together

LOST HALLWAYS

Around Sundown: The Wandering

I love you for this house you made and rearranged for 40 years,
paintings quickening the walls, migratory books in piles,
and outside, fringes of flowers and sprawling jungle grass—
all light as your light passes through

although tonight you claim that phantom house
with finer lines of vision—the art more deftly synced,
the view under stairs more shadow-striking—
and cleaner planes to hold the ceiling up,

the house you dream I cannot enter.
Mine is the one cluttered with old age detritus,
messy counters, clothes in heaps,
yours just newer, lighter,

though you must ask which door to use
and if it's dawn or night, whether we'll meet tomorrow
or next week, and if you'll need your purse.
I love you for the lamplit ghosts of songs

in poems shared and bodies flared and winged,
and say it's here, despite the clutter,
this house so like the one you dream,
but know it's lost to you at end of day,

this end of time slipping into ruin,
this garden-circled place fading into gloom

Today You Become

the many headed Hydra
saying "you've never seen
where I live," now stalking down
our road in multi-tilt
dimensions. Will you be safe?
Will your anger at my obtuseness
keep you watchful for the sudden
sweep of fender around our bend?
High dudgeon has its amplitudes
and confessions, its focus and blindness,
kicking free the shackles of insult and guilt—

the world old as we are now
who made love to the beat of ancient stones
and walked our crooked miles
of crooked seasons
lovely in their vanishings.

Her Laugh

Can Suzy come out to play
the child in me wishes to say.
Can she dance in the field,
twirl her hair in the breeze,
maybe kick up her heels,
say love as you please

as grass does the light
or the lake takes the storm?
Can she flow through the night
all liquid with form?
Oh tell me O house on the hill,
can Suzy come out to play

though dusk's come in with a chill
and taken her laughter away?

Undertow

Where is it the clock ran?
How cold the ancient entryway!
You see me in two

like a knife knifing the eye.
How wise is a mirror?
You are too many ghosts to attend to

and make for the darkest of weathers.
I feel your many-ness.
I chase your dissolve.

Maybe after a deep dive
we will come up for air
and remember.

When We Danced

Light was the dance and the dance was light
O dizzying dish of my demise,
dervish of those long-ago faded levis—
I see us still,
stark, illuminated in the chill,
a chaliced stillness in the tottering night.

Lost Hallways

The music makes you smile and stills my soul.
The past drifts back, flotsam and jetsam
of a lost treasure ship, our heroine
going down to Davy Jones—her face,
less mobile but still beautiful
and darkly haunted now.
                              I dread
the minutes like whipcracks, help you
into clothes and down lost hallways—
treat you like a toddler till you say
"I can't find my heart,
I'm just all tears and nothing else."

We Ban the News

as every wound
becomes your wound, all tears your tears.
With no capacity to distance, Ukraine
outside your window, your tribe's
the Poor, the Damaged and the Lost
among the skulls of broken cities—
a child's doll
half visible in the rubble.

Our Luck

runs out like sand through an hourglass—
your beauty once like the new-fallen snow
now shades to gray, the color of our winter's
long months to come.
       I cannot hold you
or let you go. Still days darken.
Black trees bow in wind.
        We've lost
our way in the worst of seasons
in the whorl of the guffawing crow,
our garden gone to seed, our eyes
like Homer's falling heroes'
going black.
     I remain perhaps
your last plucked flower
in the wilt of my will.

Looking for the Door

You can no longer lie down without help
and my anxiety gut tightens
and churns. I'm looking for the door
in a room without doors, my grief
god-sized and implacable.
Who can I bargain with?
Once we were shuddering
interchangeables, silvery fish
in a pod of perfect
ballet.
            Now I move you about
like an armload of lumber,
your muscles stiff with uncertainty,
your face vaguely fearful.
I yearn to give birth to you, feel you
unfold like our floppy magnolia
blossoms in spring, lavish and lovely
in their lascivious come-ons.
I long for that fluency and fiery freedom
against this hardening ossification,
this deaf call to stillness.

Our Absence

stretches out, the long haul
of a short future, the unsaying
of lost conversations, love's erasures
and grievances, half-smiles, pain groans,
night sweats. I love you, I love you, I love you
but can no longer remember
the contour of it, the smoke of it, your fire
in the quickening twilight.
I hate you, I hate you, I hate you
sing the demons of my forgetfulness.
Cursed by my myriad blessings
and the silk of your skin
I ease you into sleep.

ONCE

Once
(with some thefts from Simon Behbehani)

I came to you as if from a far country
The night was not quite in your eyes
but the evening smoke and the roses of your skin
met in purple shadows

I came through the vague veiled streets
toward some clarity or hunger
You were my fire in the moth-light
my confessor

You danced the stars blind under the witching moon
I crawled in your darkness like the tapping beetle
Our mouths met

Dawn in the desert is a million gold butterflies
I lived there once among broken stones
husks of bodies
a tale of death and deaths
and women turned to salt
under stubborn hummocks of black cloth

We grow old like the cracking clay
of forgotten rivers
Soon no one will remember our voices
or the glancing light of our tremulous
tremors

Was it the wind I came on
lipping your waters
combing the sunlight scarves across your throat
So often now we are tired
and old women I once knew speak harshly
behind the curtain
and the mud of the riverbank

squelches under their feet

I came through bulrushes over moon-glazed bayous
and our bodies became snake-dancing
cranes
feathery cries

We cannot love each other forever
except as the stars do
all flame and nothingness

Our skins will grow worn and frail
as papyrus leaves
locust wings
May the burden of pain bring lightness

We lie down to take flight
like the desert sand under the scour of wind

I came like a sea eagle out of the sun's eye
to whirl you talon in talon
down the roller coaster sky

I met your gaze in the forest of being

The rest was just history

www.ingramcontent.com/pod-product-compliance
Lightning Source LLC
Chambersburg PA
CBHW021744190726
48288CB00009B/3159

9 781733 888295